Scottish
Wit & Wisdom

The Meanings Behind Famous Scottish Sayings

Betty Kirkpatrick

Crombie Jardine
PUBLISHING LIMITED
www.crombiejardine.com

Crombie Jardine
PUBLISHING LIMITED
www.crombiejardine.com

Crombie Jardine Publishing Limited
Office 2, 3 Edgar Buildings, George Street, Bath, BA1 2FJ
www.crombiejardine.com

This edition has been produced exclusively for The Scotsman

ISBN: 978-1-906051-50-1

Designed by www.glensaville.com
Printed and bound in Great Britain

CONTENTS

INTRODUCTION

Scotland has had its fair share of comedians, both professional and self-styled, but the wit of Scotland is not traditionally of the laugh-out-loud variety. Rather it is of an understated, wry-smile type, known in Scotland as pawkie humour. The Concise Scots Dictionary defines pawkie as 'having a matter-of-fact, humorously critical outlook on life, characterized by a sly, quiet wit', which sums it up very well. Alas this dry style of humour has the disadvantage that, unlike the obvious joke, it can go unnoticed. It is partly for this reason that the Scots have acquired a reputation in some quarters of being dour or humourless, but often the fault has lain with the hearers who did not recognize wit when it was presented to them.

There is less need to explain the wisdom of the Scots, since Scotland, especially considering its size, has produced a great number of people who have made a significant contribution to the shaping of the world. These have included people from a wide range of disciplines, such as poets, philosophers, novelists, artists, architects, engineers, explorers, doctors, scientists and so on, and the thoughts of some of these are included in the following selection of sayings and quotations.

Any collection of these, especially such a short one, is bound to be extremely personal and I have decided to concentrate on the traditional and the historical. In this modern age where so much is disposable and so ephemeral, it is good, I think, to give prominence, at least occasionally, to the tried and the true.

The Scots have their own language that developed quite separately from English, although they share a common ancestor in Old English. Over the centuries, however, for various political, educational and cultural reasons, English gradually became the dominant language in Scotland, and now, though valiant efforts are being made to revive the flagging spirit of the Scots language, there are many people, especially of the younger generation, who know, at best, only a few words of it. Thus, although several of the traditional sayings in proverbs contain Scots words, these are absent from many of the quoted writers because they penned their thoughts in English.

A short glossary has been added as a guide to the Scots element in the book. In case you are puzzled over any of the spellings of Scots words, it should be remembered that Scots, unlike English and most other languages, lacks a standard spelling scheme. This inevitably gives rise to one word having several variants, making it almost impossible to misspell a Scots word.

SAGE SAYINGS & PITHY PROVERBS

HEALTH

Better wear shoon than sheets.

*It is better to wear shoes to keep the feet
warm and dry (even though this may be
expensive) rather than become ill.*

A cauld needs the cook as muckle as the doctor.

Nutritious food can cure a cold as effectively as medicine.

Feed a cauld and starve a fever.
*Traditional advice about giving nutritious
food to people suffering with a cold is not
always appropriate if they have a fever.*

Feed a cauld but hunger a colic.
*A similar sentiment to the previous
saying, where the condition not requiring
nourishment is a stomach disorder.*

Fill fu' and haud fu' maks a stark man.
Plenty of good food and drink makes a person strong.

Gae tae bed wi' the lamb and rise wi' the laverock.

A recipe for remaining healthy; a Scots version of 'early to bed, early to rise'.

He that eats but ae dish seldom needs the doctor.

A warning to be sparing in the amount of food you eat, if you want to remain healthy.

If ye want to be soon weel be lang sick.

Not a recommendation to malinger, but advice not to get out of bed too soon after you have been ill.

Licht suppers mak lang days.

*A recommendation to eat sparingly, especially in
the evening, if you wish to live to an old age.*

Rise when the day daws,
Bed when the nicht fa's.

*An injunction to stay healthy by going
to bed early and getting up early.*

Suppers kill mair than doctors cure.

*Another recommendation to eat sparingly,
especially in the evening.*

FOOD

A drap and a bit's but sma' requite.

*Said as an invitation to guests to partake
of food and drink, indicating that this is
little recompense for their friendship.*

A hungry man's an angry man.

*This speaks for itself – it is undoubtedly true that many
people become bad-tempered when they get hungry.*

A hungry man's meat is
lang o' makin' ready.

*When you're very hungry the preparation of
your food seems to take a very long time; a
similar saying to 'a watched pot never boils'.*

A hungry wame has nae lugs.

*Those who are hungry seem to lose the power
of hearing and so don't listen to reason.*

A kiss and a drink o' watter
mak a wersh breakfast.

*Said as a warning to a couple who think they
can live on love and very little else.*

As the soo fills, the draff soors.

*Literally, as the sow fills up, its food begins to taste
sour; a compliment to a host to express that the food has
been so plentiful and so good that the guest's appetite
has been fully satisfied and he/she can eat no more.*

Bannocks are better than nae breid.

Very plain food is better than no food at all; a similar
saying to 'half a loaf is better than no bread'.

Better belly burst than gude meat spoil.

It is better to eat too much than let good
food go to waste; said by those who eat too
much, as justification for their greed.

Better wait on the cook than the doctor.

A reference to the fact that many people felt that the ill
would benefit more from nourishing food than medicine,
although this could vary with the type of illness.

Breid's hoose is skailed never.

If a house contains bread you can
never say it has no food in it.

Eat in measure and defy the doctor.

Moderation in eating makes for a healthy life.

Eats meat, an's never fed; wears claes and never cled.

No matter how well-fed or well-clothed some people may be, they never seem to look any better for it.

Eat weel's drink weel's brither.

Eating well and drinking well should go together.

Fat paunches bode lean pows.

People who are greedy and over-fed have empty heads.

Hunger's good kitchen.

When you're hungry any food tastes good.

Hunger's good kitchen to a cauld potato, but a wet divot to the lowe o' love.

Hunger makes the humblest of food (such as a cold potato) seem very appetizing, but it dampens romantic passion.

I'm neither sma' drink thirsty nor grey bread hungry.

Said by someone who is disappointed at the standard of fare that he/she has been offered by a host.

●

Mennans are better than nae meat.

Both this and the saying opposite indicate that it is better to have very little food than no food at all. In Scots the word meat is often used for food in general and mennans are minnows or very small fish.

Poor folk seek meat for their stamacks and rich folk seek stamacks for their meat.

The poor eat because they're hungry, the rich because they feel they have to, even if they have little appetite.

●

Naething sooner maks a man auld-like than fitting ill to his meat.

Nothing ages people so rapidly as being ill-fed.

Ne'er gie' me death in a toom dish.

A jocular saying used by people who like their food and want some of it, literally meaning 'don't give me death by means of an empty dish, don't starve me to death'.

Ne'er speak ill o' them whose breid ye eat.

A warning not to criticize your host.

Mennans are better than nae fish.

See the saying on the previous page.

O' a' the meat in the warld,
the drink gaes best doon.

*This speaks for itself in a land that
makes and loves whisky.*

Some hae meat and canna eat
And some wad meat that want it
But we hae meat and we can eat,
For which the Lord be thankit.

A grace said before meals, known as the Selkirk Grace.

They may ken by your beard what
has been on your board.

*A way of telling someone that some of the food he
has just eaten is stuck on his beard or chin.*

The nearer the grave, the greedier.

The older people get, the more food they like to have.

Stuffin' hauds oot storms.

Advice given to people who are setting out on a journey in bad weather to eat well before they leave.

Welcome's the best dish in the kitchen.

Food given with a good will tastes the best.

They hae need o'a canny cook that hae but ae egg to their denner.

It takes a clever, ingenious cook to make a meal out of very little; also extended to mean that it takes a resourceful person to make the most of what is to hand.

Tak a piece – your teeth's longer than your beard.

Words of encouragement said to children to get them to take a titbit or treat when they have the chance.

17

**Ye hae tint your ain stamack
an' found a tyke's.**

*A remark made to someone who is eating
a great deal as though very hungry.*

**Your meat will mak you bonny and
when you're bonny you'll be well
lo'ed and when you're well lo'ed you'll
be licht-hearted and when you're
licht-hearted you'll loup far.**

Said to children to encourage them to eat.

**What's in your wame's no
in your testament.**

*Said as an encouragement to someone to eat up; a
reminder that if you eat everything on your plate
you cannot leave it to someone else in your will.*

When all fruit fa's, welcome ha's.

*When we have consumed all the finer food,
we must be content with the plain kind.*

WEATHER

About the moon there is a brough,
The weather will be cold and rough.
A warning of rough weather if there is
a halo effect round the moon.

A green Yule maks a fat kirkyard.
A wet winter results in many deaths because of the many
illnesses that are caused or worsened by damp conditions.

As the day lengthens, the
cauld strengthens.
A reminder that when the days begin to get
longer, the weather often becomes colder.

Cast not a clout till May be oot.

Often taken to mean that people should not remove any of their winter clothing until the month of May has passed. However, it is thought by some that May refers to the hawthorn, the advice being not to remove any winter clothes until the hawthorn is in blossom.

East and wast the sign o' a blast; north and south, the sign o' a drouth.

A saying that uses the direction of the prevailing wind to forecast the weather.

If Candlemas Day be dry and fair
The hauf o' winter's to come and mair.
If Candlemas Day be wet and foul,
The hauf o' winter's gaun at Yule.

Candlemas Day is February 2 and it was taken as a good weather sign if it was wet on that day.

E'ening grey an' a morning red, put on your hat or ye'll wet your head. E'ening red an' a morning grey, is a taiken o' a bonny day.

A weather saying with a similar meaning to 'red sky at night, shepherd's delight, red sky in the morning, shepherd's warning'.

If grass grows green in Janaveer, it will be the waur for it a' the year.

The belief was that if the grass was green too early in the year, it was unlikely to survive the rest of the year.

Mony haws, mony snaws.

A warning that a good harvest of haw berries will result in a cold, hard winter.

**Mist in May
and heat in June make
the harvest right soon.**
A self-evident weather saying.

**Sorrow an' ill weather
come unca'd.**
*Both ill fortune and ill weather
are beyond our control.*

**The rain cams scouth, when
the wind's i' the south.**
*In this context scouth means freely,
without restraint, and so the saying indicates
that heavy rain will occur when there
a wind blowing from the south.*

When the moon is on her back
Gae mend your shoon and
sort your thack.

When the moon appears in such a position,
it should be seen as a sign of rain, and
appropriate measures should be taken.

Under water dearth,
under snaw bread.

A field that has been flooded with water
will produce a very poor crop, but one
that has been covered in snow will
produce a good one.

MONEY

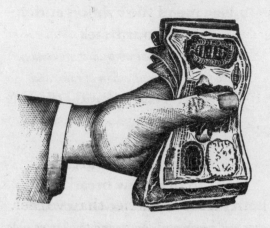

A' complain o' want o' siller, but nane o' want o' sense.

A saying indicating that desiring more money is a far more common human preoccupation than desiring more sense.

A deaf man will hear the clink o' money.

A saying that emphasizes the lure of money very well.

Get what you can, and keep what you hae, that's the way to get rich.
It sounds so easy that it makes you wonder why there are not more rich people around!

A fu' sack can bear a clout i' the side.
A prosperous person can afford to take a few knocks from fate.

Better a tocher in her than wi' her.
A tocher was a woman's dowry and this saying suggests that it was better for a woman to have good qualities within, rather than have a lot of money and possessions.

Gathering gear is weel-liket wark.
Acquiring money is generally thought to be a pleasant occupation.

He's got his nose in a gude kail pat.
*Literally, he has got his head in a good soup pot; said
of a person who has married someone well-off.*

He wad rake hell for a bodle.
*A saying indicating how much someone loves money and
what a miser he is, a bodle being an old copper coin.*

Eaten meat is ill to pay.
*No one likes to have to pay for something
that has already been consumed.*

Lay your wame to your winning.
A warning not to consume more than you earn.

It's folly to live poor to dee rich.
*The moral is self-evident, akin to
'you can't take it with you'.*

●

Moyen does muckle, but moyen does mair.
Influence can do a lot, but money is even more powerful.

There are nane sae weel shod but may slip.

*Everyone, including the wealthy, is at
risk from misfortune and mishaps.*

He wad skin a louse for the tallow.

A saying that describes just how miserly someone is.

**It's as easy to get siller frae a lawyer
as butter frae a black dog's hause.**

*Hause means throat in this instance, so the saying suggests
that acquiring silver from a lawyer is an impossible feat.*

Wealth gars wits waver.

*People tend to lose their common sense
when money is involved.*

Wealth has made mair men covetous than covetousness has made men wealthy.

A warning against greed.

The siller penny slays mair souls than the nakit sword slays bodies.

A comment on the destructive power of money.

Put twa pennies in a purse and they will creep thigither.

A saying indicating how money soon accumulates if you save it.

Want o' wit is waur than want o' gear.

It is worse to be lacking in intelligence and sense than to be lacking in money.

SILENCE

A close mou catches nae flees.

A recommendation to say as little as possible; a variation on 'shut your mouth and you'll get no flies'.

Ah dinna bile ma cabbages twice.

Said as a refusal to repeat what has just been said; literally 'I don't boil my cabbages twice'.

Dinna open yer mou tae fill ither fowks.

A warning not to gossip.

**Gie yer tongue mair holidays
than yer heid.**

*An imaginative way of suggesting that people
should think more than they speak.*

Keep yer mou shut and yer een open.

*A warning that you will learn more if
you say little and observe a lot.*

Keep your breath tae cool yer parritch.

A piece of advice given to someone who is wasting words.

He that spares to speak, spares to speed.

*A saying not in favour of silence, but one that suggests that
people who don't point out their own talents don't succeed.*

**Keep yer gab steekit when
ye kenna yer company.**

*A warning not to say too much in front of
strangers; literally to keep your mouth closed
when you don't know who is present.*

Put your thoom on that!
Literally, put your thumb on that; said as
a warning to keep something secret.

Pint stoups hae lang lugs.
A reminder that those who drink too
much often say too much.

The loodest bummer's no the best bee.
The person who says the most is rarely
the most effective person.

When a' men speak, nae man hears.
If everyone speaks at once, no one hears
or takes in anything that is said.

Think mair than ye say.

Devote more time to thought than speech.

●

Wide lugs and a short tongue are best.

It is best to listen a lot and say very little.

Wae is the wife that wants a tongue, but weel's the man that gat her.

It is unfortunate to be a woman who says very little, since little notice will be taken of her, but it is fortunate to be a man who marries such a woman.

●

TRUTH

A fu' heart never lied.

*People are more likely to tell the truth
when they are in the grip of emotion.*

●

Auld saws speak truths.

*There's a lot of truth in old sayings,
as this collection proves.*

●

Craft maun hae claes, but truth gangs nakit.

*Cunning may be disguised, but truth does
not need any cover or embellishment.*

Facts are chiels that winna ding.

Facts, and therefore the truth,
cannot be denied.

He never lies, but when the holly's green.

Since holly is an evergreen tree, this saying indicates
that the person in question never tells the truth.

If a'thing's true, that's nae lee.

A saying used to express disbelief in
what has just been said.

It's a sin to lee on the diel.

You should always speak the truth, even
where wicked people are concerned.

Truth and honesty keep the croon on the causey.

People who are honest and truthful stay out of trouble. The 'croon o' the causey' or the crown of the causeway was the highest part of the street, farthest way from the gutter where all the rubbish gathered.

Truth will stand when a'thing's failin'.

Truth can be relied upon when everything else fails.

WORDS

A' are no freens that speak us fair.
*Just because someone pays you a compliment
or says something nice about you, you cannot
assume that he/she is your friend.*

●

A' his buzz shaks nae barley.
*Said of someone who may say a great deal but
whose words have no effect on the situation.*

●

A man o' words but no' o' deeds is like a garden fu' o' weeds.

A saying telling us that actions are much more useful than mere words.

●

Bairns speak i' the field whit they hear i' the ha'.

A warning to parents to be careful what they say in front of their children in case what was uttered in private is repeated in public.

Muckle spoken, part spilt.

Said of a subject which has been talked about to such an extent that much of its meaning has been lost or ignored.

Praise without profit puts little i' the pat.

Fine words alone are not much practical use to anyone.

Glib i' the tongue is aye glaikit at the heart.

Another saying that warns against being impressed or taken in by the flattery of smooth-talking people, as they are very likely to be insincere.

Words are but wind, but dunts are the devil.

Physical blows are much worse than verbal abuse.

Fair words winna mak the pot boil.

A saying that stresses the inadequacy of mere words.

Bees that hae honey in their mouths hae stings in their tails.

A warning to be wary of people who are particularly eloquent or flattering, as they may be up to no good.

●

There's a word in my wame, but it's o'er far down.

A saying used by someone to indicate that he/ she cannot think of the right word at that moment; similar to having a word on the tip of your tongue.

**Sticks and stanes may brak my banes,
but names will never hurt me.**

*A saying indicating that, although physical abuse
may do harm to someone, verbal insults will not;
often used by schoolchildren to their tormentors.*

Thanks winna feed the cat.

*Verbal thanks is not worth much; sometimes said as a
grudging, belittling acknowledgement of spoken thanks.*

Ye wad wheedle a laverock frae the lift.

*Said to someone who is particularly charming
or persuasive, as though they are able to
persuade the lark to leave the sky.*

**It's a gude tongue that says nae ill,
but a better heart that thinks none.**

*A self-evident saying that praises the
harbouring of charitable thoughts.*

QUOTATIONS

John Logie Baird (1888–1946)

television pioneer

✳✳✳✳✳✳✳✳✳✳✳✳✳✳✳✳

Seeing by wireless.

A definition of television ascribed to him

Lady Frances Balfour (1858–1931)
writer and suffragist

Golf has ceased to be a peculiarly national game. It is now no longer a pastime for the impecunious Scot, armed with two or three clubs, and a feather ball, it has become a professional sport, pursued by devastating hordes of foreigners among whom the American tongue rises shrill and strident.

Ne Obliviscaris: Dinna Forget (1930)

J. M. Barrie (1860–1937)
playwright and novelist

We are undoubtedly a sentimental people, and it sometimes plays havoc with that other celebrated sense of ours, the practical.

From a speech to the Royal Scottish Corporation on 30 November 1928

James Boswell (1740–95)

biographer of Samuel Johnson

We cannot tell the precise moment when friendship is formed. As in filling a vessel drop by drop, there is at last a drop that makes it run over; so in a series of kindnesses, there is at last one which makes the heart run over.

Life of Samuel Johnson (1791)

John Buchan (1875–1940)

writer and statesman

The dominant thought of youth is the bigness of the world, of age its smallness. As we grow older we escape from the tyranny of matter and recognize that the true centre of gravity is the mind.

Memory Hold-the-Door (1941)

ROBERT BURNS (1759–96)
poet and song-writer

Princes and lords are but the breath of kings,
'An honest man's the noblest work o' God'.

The Cotter's Saturday Night (1785) –
Burns quotes Alexander Pope

The best-laid schemes o' mice and men
Gang aft agley, An' leave us nought but
grief an' pain, For promis'd joy!

To a Mouse (1785) – oft-quoted lines commenting
on the essential fallibility of plans and hopes

Then gently scan your brother Man,
Still gentler sister woman, Tho' they may gang a
kennin' wrang, To step aside is human.

Address to the Unco' Guid (1786) – lines that urge people to
refrain from passing judgement on others

O wad some Power the giftie gie us
To see oursels as ithers see us!
It wad frae monie a blunder free us,
An' foolish notion.

To a Louse (1786) – a poem written when he saw such
a creature on a lady's hat in church, with lines indicating
that we would not behave so foolishly if we could view
ourselves with the eyes of others

But pleasures are like poppies spread, You seize the flower, its bloom is shed, Or like the snow falls in the river, A moment white – then melts forever.

Tam o' Shanter (1790) – lines indicating that Burns could be lyrical in English as well as Scots

Then let us pray that come it may, As come it will, for a' that, That sense and worth, o'er a' the earth' Shall bear the gree, an a' that; For a' that and a' that, It's comin' yet for a' that, That man to man the world o'er, Shall brothers be for a' that.

For a' that and a' that (1795)

Thomas Carlyle
(1795–1881)
historian and essayist

In the long run every Government is
the exact symbol of its People, with
their wisdom and their unwisdom;
we have to say,
Like People like Government.

Past and Present (1843)

A well-written Life is almost
as rare as a well-spent one.

Critical and Miscellaneous Essays (1838)

If Jesus Christ were to come today, people
would not even crucify him. They would ask
him to dinner, and hear what he had to say,
and make fun of it.

Carlyle at His Zenith (1927) by D. A. Wilson

ANDREW CARNEGIE (1835–1919)
industrialist and philanthropist

There is an unwritten law among the
best workmen: 'Thou shalt not take thy
neighbour's job.'

Forum (August 1886)

Golf is an indispensable adjunct to
high civilization.

Said when leaving a large sum of money to
Yale University to build a golf course

LORD HENRY COCKBURN (1779–1854)

judge

◇◇◇◇◇◇◇◇

I never see a scene of Scotch beauty, without
being thankful that I have beheld it before
it has been breathed over by the angel of
mechanical destruction.

Circuit Journeys (1847)

Sir Arthur Conan Doyle (1859–1930)
novelist – creator of Sherlock Holmes

It is a capital mistake to theorize before one has data. Insensibly one begins to twist facts to suit theories, instead of theories to suit facts.

A Scandal in Bohemia (1891)

Sir Alexander Fleming (1881–1955)
bacteriologist and discoverer of penicillin

This thirst for immediate results is by no means uncommon, but it is extremely harmful. Really valuable research is a long-term affair.

The Life of Sir Alexander Fleming (1959) by André Maurois

A good gulp of whisky at bedtime – it's not very scientific, but it helps.

A remedy for the common cold ascribed to him

Sir Patrick Geddes (1854–1932)
townplanner and biologist

When an idea is dead it is embalmed in a textbook.
The Worlds of Patrick Geddes (1978) by Philip Boardman

(James) Keir Hardie (1856–1915)
Labour politician

I think it could be shown that the position of women, as of most other things, has always been better, nearer to equality, with man, in Celtic, than in non-Celtic, races.

DAVID HUME (1711–76)
philosopher and historian

The great end of all human industry is the attainment of happiness. For this were arts invented, science cultivated, laws ordained and societies modelled by the most profound wisdom of patriots and legislators.

Essays: Moral, Political and Literary, 'The Stoic' (1742)

DAVID LIVINGSTONE (1813–73)
missionary and explorer

The strangest thing I have seen in this country seems really to be broken-heartedness and it attacks free men who have been captured and made slaves.

Last Journal of David Livingstone in Central Africa (1874)

Hugh McDiarmid, pseudonym of Christopher Grieve (1892–1978)

poet

◇◇◇◇◇◇◇◇

There is so much that is bad in all the poetry
that Scots people know and admire that it is not
surprising that for their pet example of a good
bad poet they should have to go outside the range
of poetry, good, bad, or indifferent altogether.
McGonagall is in a very special category, and has it
entirely to himself.

Scottish Eccentrics (1936)

Charles Rennie Mackintosh (1868–1928)

architect and designer

◇◇◇◇◇◇◇◇◇◇◇◇◇◇◇◇◇◇◇◇◇◇◇◇◇◇◇

Don't meddle with other people's ideas
when you have all the work cut out of you in
trying to express your own.

Seemliness (1902)

JOHN MUIR (1838–1914)
naturalist and founder of the
American Natural Park system

Wherever a Scotsman goes, there goes Burns.
His grand whole, catholic soul squares with
the good of all; therefore we find him in
everything everywhere.

John of the Mountains (1938), edited by I. M. Wolfe

MARGARET OLIPHANT (1828–97)
novelist and critic

Life is no definite thing with a beginning
and an end, a growth and a climax; but a basket
of fragments, passages that lead to nothing,
curious incidents which look of importance at
first, but which crumble and break into
pieces, dropping into ruins.

Review of Henry James's
A London Life in *Backwoods' Edinburgh Magazine* (1888)

Sir Walter Scott (1771–1832)
novelist and poet

∞∞∞∞∞∞∞∞∞∞∞∞∞∞∞∞∞∞∞

Oh, what a tangled web we weave, When first we practise to deceive!

Marmion (1808)

I make it a rule to cheat nobody but booksellers, a race on whom I have no mercy.

Letter to Thomas Sheridan (1811)

To live the life of an author for mere bread is perhaps the most dreadful fate than can be encountered.

Letter to James Bailey (June 1817)

Many a clever boy is flogged into a dunce and many an original composition corrected into mediocrity.

Journal (June 1826)

But who cares for the whipped cream
of London society?

Journal (April 1828)

Surely chess-playing is a sad waste of brains.

Memoirs of the Life of Walter Scott (1837–8) by J. G. Lockhart

SAMUEL SMILES (1812–1904)
social reformer and moralist

That terrible Nobody! How much has he to
answer for. More mischief is done by Nobody
than by all the world besides.

Thrift (1875)

ADAM SMITH (1723–90)

economist and philosopher

It is not from the benevolence of the butcher, the brewer, or the baker, that we expect our dinner, but from their regard to their own interest.

An Inquiry into the Nature and Causes of the Wealth of Nations (1776)

ALEXANDER SMITH (1829–67)

poet

It is not of so much consequence what you say, as how you say it. Memorable sentences are memorable on account of some single irradiating word.

'On the Writing of Essays', Dreamthorp (1863)

Tobias Smollett (1721–71)

novelist

◇◇◇◇◇◇◇◇◇

London is the devil's drawing-room.

The Adventures of Roderick Random (1748)

William Soutar (1898–1943)

poet and diarist

◇◇◇◇◇◇◇◇◇◇◇◇◇◇◇

Life is no loving father, but a force with which we
must contend and to which we must adapt the self.

Diary entry (June 1932)

ROBERT LOUIS STEVENSON (1850–94)

novelist, poet and essayist

For my own part, I travel not to go anywhere, but to go. I travel for travel's sake.

Travels with a Donkey (1879)

From *Virginibus Puerisque* (1881):

Even if we take marriage at its lowest, even if we regard it as no more than a sort of friendship recognized by the police.

You can read Kant by yourself if you wanted, but you must share a joke with someone else. Books are good enough in their own way, but they are a mighty bloodless substitute for life.

It is better to lose health like a spendthrift than to waste it like a miser. It is better to live and be done with it than to die daily in the sick room.

●

From *Memories and Portraits* (1887):

The first step for all is to learn to the very dregs our own ignoble fallibility. Faith means holding the same opinions as the person employing the word.

●

Marriage is one long conversation, chequered by disputes.

●

Scientific men, who imagine that their science affords an answer to the problem of existence, are perhaps the most to be pitied of mankind; and contemned.

To travel hopefully is a better
thing than to arrive.

●

JAMES THOMSON (1700–48)

poet

Poor is the triumph o'er the timid hare!

The Seasons, 'Spring' (1746)

JAMES WATT (1736-1819)

engineer and inventor

I think that I shall not long have anything to
do with the House of Commons again – I never
saw so many wrong-headed people on all sides
gathered together.

Letter to his wife (1767)

GLOSSARY

a'	all
ae	one
afore	before
aft	often
agley	awry, wrong
ah	I
an'	and
auld	old
bairn	child
bane	bone
bannock	an unleavened cake
bile	boil
breid	bread
brither	brother
bummer	a creature that makes a buzzing noise, a bee
canna	cannot
canny	careful
cauld	cold
chiel	young man, fellow
claes	clothes
cled	clad
clout	cloth
croon	crown
dee	die
deil	devil
denner	dinner
ding	deal blows, defeat
dinna	don't
doon	down
draff	pig-food
drap	drop
drouth	drought, thirst
dunt	blow
een	eyes
fa'	fall
flee	fly

fowk	folk
frae	from
freen	friend
fu'	full
gab	mouth
gae	go
gang	go
gaun	going
gear	wealth
gie	give
giftie	gift
glaikit	playful, foolish
gree	agree
gude	good
guid	good
ha'	haw, hall
hae	have
haud	hold
hauf	half
hause	throat
heid	head
het	hot
i'	in
ither	other
Janaveer	January
kail	soup; kale
kenna	don't know
kennin'	a little bit
kirk	church
kitchen	relish
lang	long
laverock	lark
lee	lie, to tell lies
licht	light
lift	sky
lo'ed	loved
loodest	loudest
lowe	flame
lowp	leap
lug	ear

mair	more
mak	make
maun	must
meat	food
mennan	minnow
monie, mony	many
mou	mouth
moyen	influence
muckle	much, large
nae	no
naething	nothing
nakit	naked
nicht	night
no'	not
o'	of
oot	out
parritch	porridge
pat	pot
piece	piece of bread, sandwich
pow	head
rin	run
shak	shake
shoon	shoes
siller	silver
skail	empty, spill
sma'	small
snaw	snow
soo	sow
soor	sour
stamack	stomach
stark	strong
steekit	closed
stoup	flagon, jug
tae	to
taiken	token
tak	take
thack	thatch
thankit	thanked
thigither	together
thoom	thumb

tint	lost
toom	empty
tyke	dog
unca'd	uncalled
wad	would
wame	stomach
wark	work
warld	world
wast	west
watter	water
waur	worse
weel	well
wersh	tasteless
whit	what
winna	won't
wrang	wrong